SOLIDS

Aaron Carr

www.av2books.com

LET'S READ
AV²
BY WEIGL™
ADDED VALUE • AUDIO VISUAL

Go to **www.av2books.com**, and enter this book's unique code.

BOOK CODE

J586176

AV² by Weigl brings you media enhanced books that support active learning.

AV² provides enriched content that supplements and complements this book. Weigl's AV² books strive to create inspired learning and engage young minds in a total learning experience.

Your AV² Media Enhanced books come alive with...

Audio
Listen to sections of the book read aloud.

Video
Watch informative video clips.

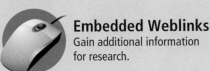

Embedded Weblinks
Gain additional information for research.

Try This!
Complete activities and hands-on experiments.

Key Words
Study vocabulary, and complete a matching word activity.

Quizzes
Test your knowledge.

Slide Show
View images and captions, and prepare a presentation.

... and much, much more!

Published by AV² by Weigl
350 5th Avenue, 59th Floor New York, NY 10118
Website: www.av2books.com   www.weigl.com

Library of Congress Cataloguing in Publication data available upon request.
Fax 1-866-449-3445 for the attention of the Publishing Records department.

ISBN 978-1-61913-601-4 (hard cover)
ISBN 978-1-61913-606-9 (soft cover)

Printed in the United States of America in North Mankato, Minnesota
1 2 3 4 5 6 7 8 9 16 15 14 13 12

062012
WEP170512

Editor: Aaron Carr   Design: Mandy Christiansen

Weigl acknowledges Getty Images, iStock, and Dreamstime as image suppliers for this title.

What is Matter?

SOLIDS

CONTENTS

Solids keep their shape.

Solids take up space.

4

Many things are solids.

Solids can be hard.

Solids can be soft.

6

Many foods are solids.

Solids can be many colors.

Solids can be many sizes and shapes.

8

Candy can be many colors, sizes, and shapes.

9

Solids can feel different from other solids.

The way a solid feels is called texture.

Many solids have texture.

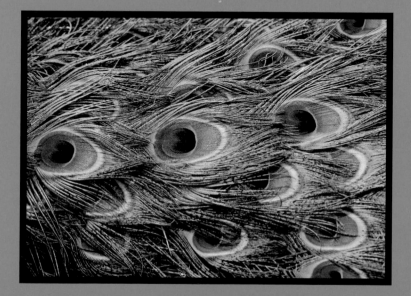 

Solids are one kind of matter.

Liquids and gases
are other kinds of matter.

There are many solids, liquids, and gases.

Solids turn to liquids when they get hot.

This is called melting.

**Ice cream melts
when it gets hot.**

 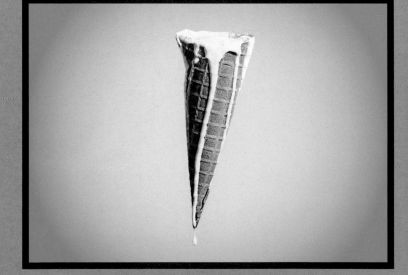

15

Liquids turn to solids when they get cold.

This is called freezing.

Water freezes
when it gets cold.

The Sun heats the air.

The Sun keeps solids warm.

The Sun helps turn ice into water.

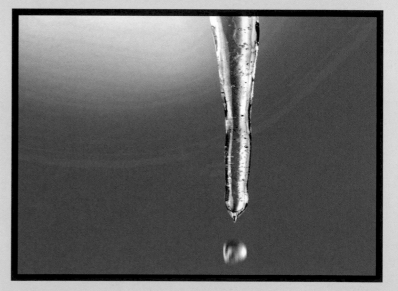

Water is an important kind of matter.

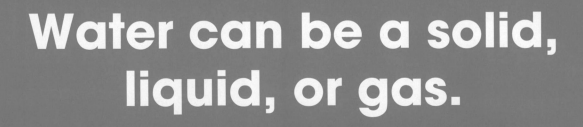

Water can be a solid, liquid, or gas.

Many things are made of water.

Everything around you is made of matter.
Which of these things is a solid?
Are any of them liquids or gases?

Can you sort these solids by color, size, or shape?

KEY WORDS

Research has shown that as much as 65 percent of all written material published in English is made up of 300 words. These 300 words cannot be taught using pictures or learned by sounding them out. They must be recognized by sight. This book contains 46 common sight words to help young readers improve their reading fluency and comprehension. This book also teaches young readers several important content words. These words are paired with pictures to aid in learning and improve understanding.

Page	Sight Words First Appearance
4	are, keep, many, take, their, things, up
6	be, can, foods, hard
8	and
10	a, different, from, have, other, the, way
12	kind, of, one, other, there
14	get, is, it, they, this, to, when
16	water
18	air, helps, into
20	an, important, made, or
22	any, around, by, them, these, which, you

Page	Content Words First Appearance
4	shape, solids, space
8	candy, colors, sizes
10	texture
12	gases, liquids, matter
14	ice cream, melting
16	freezing
18	ice, Sun
22	everything